W9-AUY-279

FORT SMALLWOOD ELEMENTARY SCHOOL
MEDIA CENTER
1720 POPLAR RIDGE ROAD
PASADENA, MARYLAND 21122

HOW TO DRAW
ROBOTS

Mark Bergin

PowerKiDS
press

New York

Published in 2009 by The Rosen Publishing Group, Inc.
29 East 21st Street, New York, NY 10010

Copyright © 2009 The Salariya Book Company Ltd.

All rights reserved. No part of this book may be reproduced in
any form without permission in writing from the publisher,
except by a reviewer.

Editor: Rob Walker
U.S. Editor: Kara Murray

Library of Congress Cataloging-in-Publication Data

Bergin, Mark.
  Robots / Mark Bergin. — 1st ed.
     p. cm. — (How to draw)
  Includes index.
   ISBN 978-1-4358-2521-5 (library binding)
ISBN 978-1-4358-2650-2 (pbk)
ISBN 978-1-4358-2662-5 (6-pack)
  1. Robots in art—Juvenile literature. 2. Drawing—Technique—
Juvenile literature. I. Title.
  NC825.R56B47 2009
  743'.89629892—dc22

                            2008010579

Manufactured in China

Contents

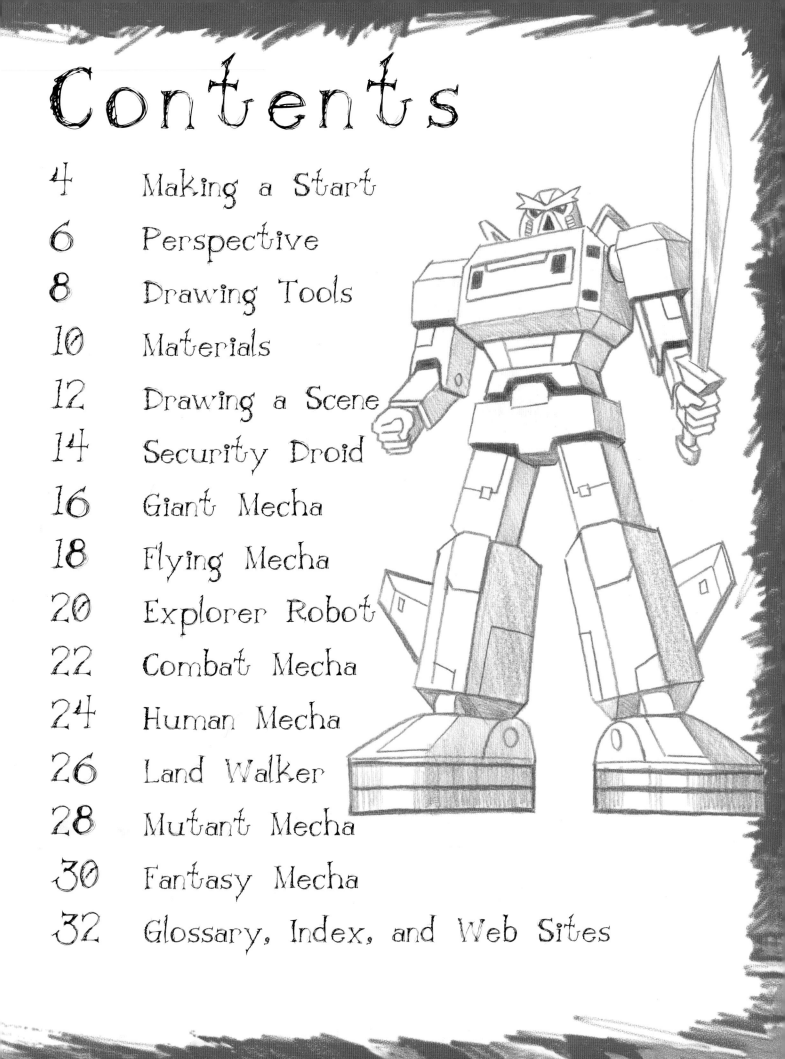

Making a Start

Learning to draw is about looking and seeing. Keep practicing and get to know your subject. Use a sketchbook to make quick sketches. Start by doodling, and experiment with shapes and patterns. There are many ways to draw. This book shows one method. Visit art galleries, look at artists' drawings, see how friends draw, but above all, find your own way.

Combat mecha

Remember that practice makes perfect. If it looks wrong, start again. Keep working at it. The more you draw, the more you will learn.

Security droid

Giant mecha

Flying mecha

Fantasy mecha

5

Perspective

If you look at any object from different viewpoints, you will see that the part that is closest to you will look larger, and the part farthest away from you will look smaller. Drawing in perspective is a way of creating a feeling of space — of showing three dimensions on a flat surface.

A view from above can be achieved using a single vanishing point.

The vanishing point (V.P.) is the place in a perspective drawing where parallel lines appear to meet. The position of the vanishing point depends on the viewer's eye level. Sometimes a low viewpoint can give your drawing added drama.

V.P.

V.P.

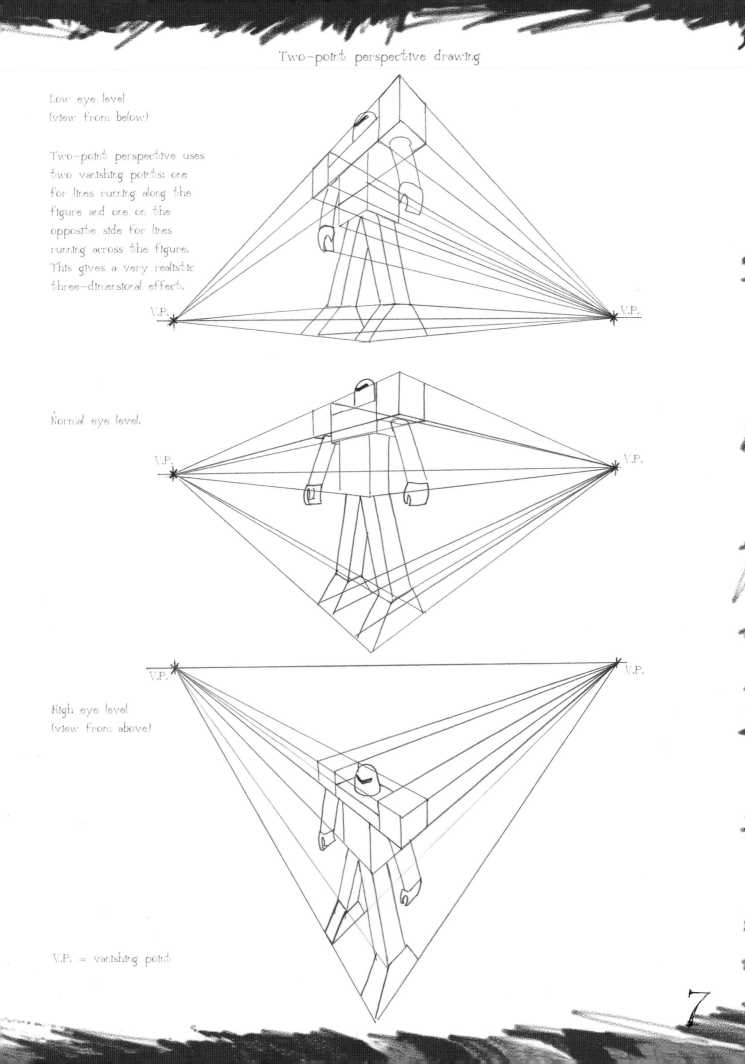

Low eye level
(view from below)

Two-point perspective uses
two vanishing points: one
for lines running along the
figure and one on the
opposite side for lines
running across the figure.
This gives a very realistic
three-dimensional effect.

V.P.

V.P.

Normal eye level.

V.P.

V.P.

V.P.

V.P.

High eye level
(view from above)

V.P. = vanishing point

Drawing Tools

Here are just a few of the many tools that you can use for drawing. Let your imagination go, and have fun experimenting with all the different marks you can make.

Each grade of **pencil** makes a different mark, from fine, gray lines to soft, black ones. Pencils are graded from #1 (the softest) to #4 (the hardest).

Watercolor pencils come in many different colors and make a line similar to #2 pencil. Paint over your finished drawing with clean water, and the lines will soften and run.

It is less messy and easier to achieve a fine line with a **charcoal pencil** than a charcoal stick. Create soft tones by smudging lines with your finger. Ask an adult to spray the drawing with fixative to prevent further smudging.

Pastels are brittle sticks of powdered color. They blend and smudge easily and are ideal for quick sketches. Pastel drawings work well on textured, colored paper. Ask an adult to spray your finished drawing with fixative.

Experiment with **finger painting**. Your fingerprints make exciting patterns and textures. Use your fingers to smudge soft pencil, charcoal, and pastel lines.

8

Ballpoint pens are very useful for sketching and making notes. Make different tones by building up layers of shading.

A **mapping pen** has to be dipped into bottled ink to fill the nib. Different nib shapes make different marks. Try putting a diluted ink wash over parts of the finished drawing.

Drafting pens and specialist **art pens** can produce extremely fine lines and are ideal for creating surface texture. A variety of pen nibs are available which produce different line widths.

Felt—tip pens are ideal for quick sketches. If the ink is not waterproof, try drawing on wet paper and see what happens.

Broad—ribbed **marker pens** make interesting lines and are good for large, bold sketches. Try using a black pen for the main sketch and a gray one to block in areas of shadow.

Paintbrushes are shaped differently to make different marks. Japanese brushes are soft and produce beautiful flowing lines. Large sable brushes are good for painting a wash over a line drawing. Fine brushes are good for drawing delicate lines.

Materials

Try using different types of drawing papers and materials. Experiment with charcoal, wax crayons, and pastels. All pens, from felt-tips to ballpoints, will make interesting marks. Try drawing with pen and ink on wet paper.

Ink silhouette

Felt-tips come in a range of line widths. The wider pens are good for filling in large areas of flat tone.

Remember, the best equipment and materials will not necessarily make the best drawing — practice will!

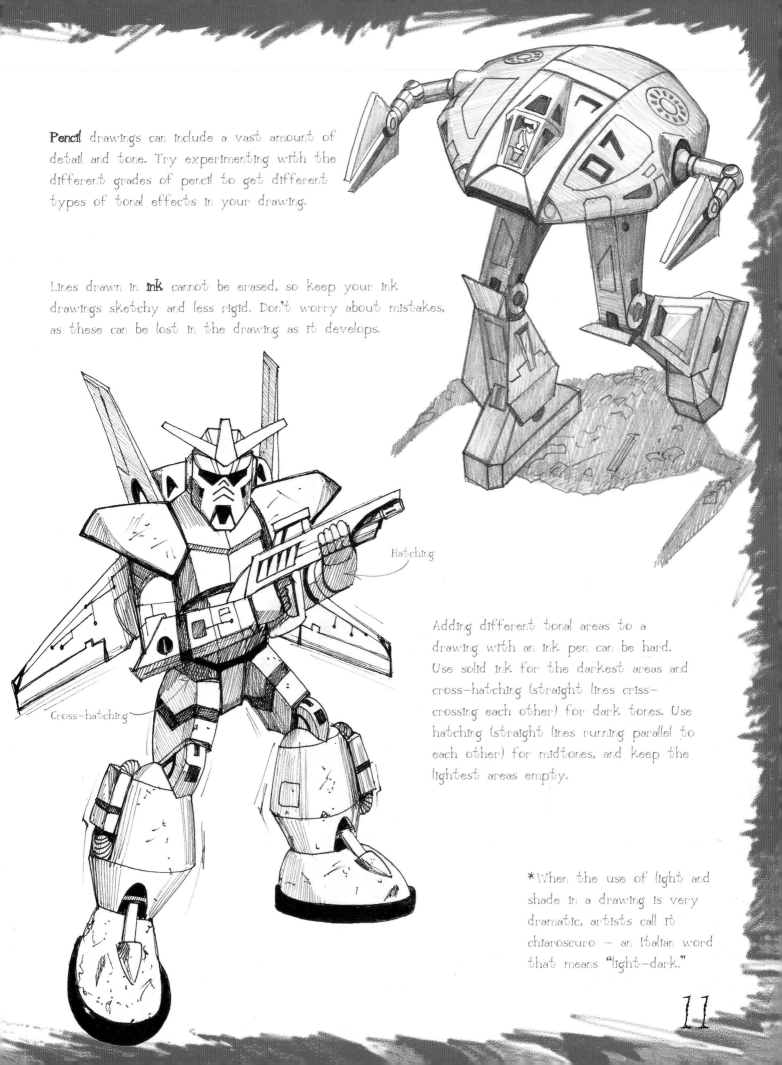

Pencil drawings can include a vast amount of detail and tone. Try experimenting with the different grades of pencil to get different types of tonal effects in your drawing.

Lines drawn in **ink** cannot be erased, so keep your ink drawings sketchy and less rigid. Don't worry about mistakes, as these can be lost in the drawing as it develops.

Hatching

Cross-hatching

Adding different tonal areas to a drawing with an ink pen can be hard. Use solid ink for the darkest areas and cross-hatching (straight lines criss-crossing each other) for dark tones. Use hatching (straight lines running parallel to each other) for midtones, and keep the lightest areas empty.

*When the use of light and shade in a drawing is very dramatic, artists call it chiaroscuro — an Italian word that means "light-dark."

11

Drawing a Scene

To make your mecha robot drawing even more exciting, you can place the mecha in a scene. This can give your drawing added drama and a sense of action. This example shows the mecha robots in a cityscape, but you can use your imagination to draw them in any situation you like.

First draw a box with a horizon line running through it, then draw the construction lines of the mecha robots themselves. Any vanishing points (see page 6) should be on the horizon line.

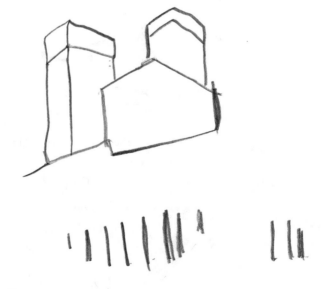

Use the horizon line and perspective to draw the square shapes of the city buildings. Add detail to the mecha robots. Sketch in simple shapes for objects, such as cars and people.

Once you have the basic shape of the drawing, you can start to add windows to the buildings and put in the final details on the bodies of the mecha robots.

13

Security Droid

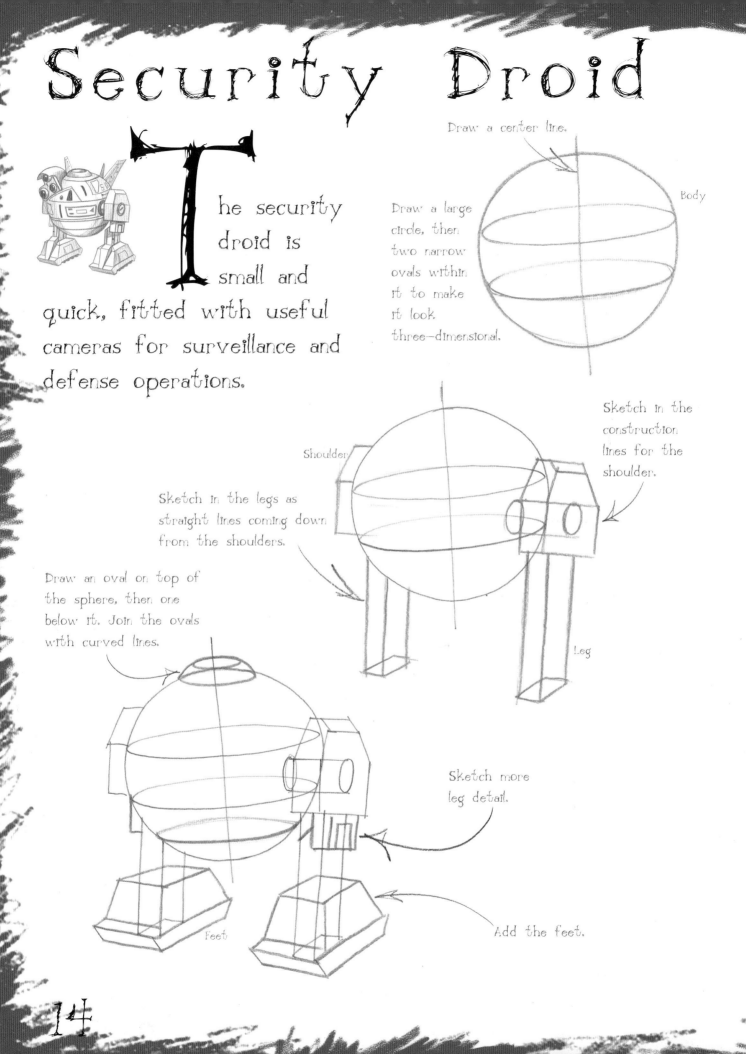

T he security droid is small and quick, fitted with useful cameras for surveillance and defense operations.

Draw a center line.

Body

Draw a large circle, then two narrow ovals within it to make it look three-dimensional.

Sketch in the construction lines for the shoulder.

Shoulder

Sketch in the legs as straight lines coming down from the shoulders.

Draw an oval on top of the sphere, then one below it. Join the ovals with curved lines.

Leg

Sketch more leg detail.

Feet

Add the feet.

A curved line coming from the top of the robot marks the top of the camera unit.

Draw ovals for the lenses of the camera unit.

Draw rectangles and lines on the body. Remember to curve the lines to keep it looking spherical.

Camera unit

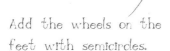

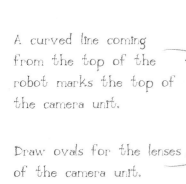

The fins on the rear of the robot are drawn with straight lines, forming an almost triangular shape.

Wheels

Add the wheels on the feet with semicircles.

This detail looks a little like circuit boards. Add some to your drawing to make it look more robotic.

Shade in the lenses of the cameras, adding a highlight to each one for the reflection in the glass.

Shade in the areas where light will not reach.

Complete the detail of the feet.

Complete the shoulders of the security robot.

The straight edges make shading the darkest areas easier.

15

Giant Mecha

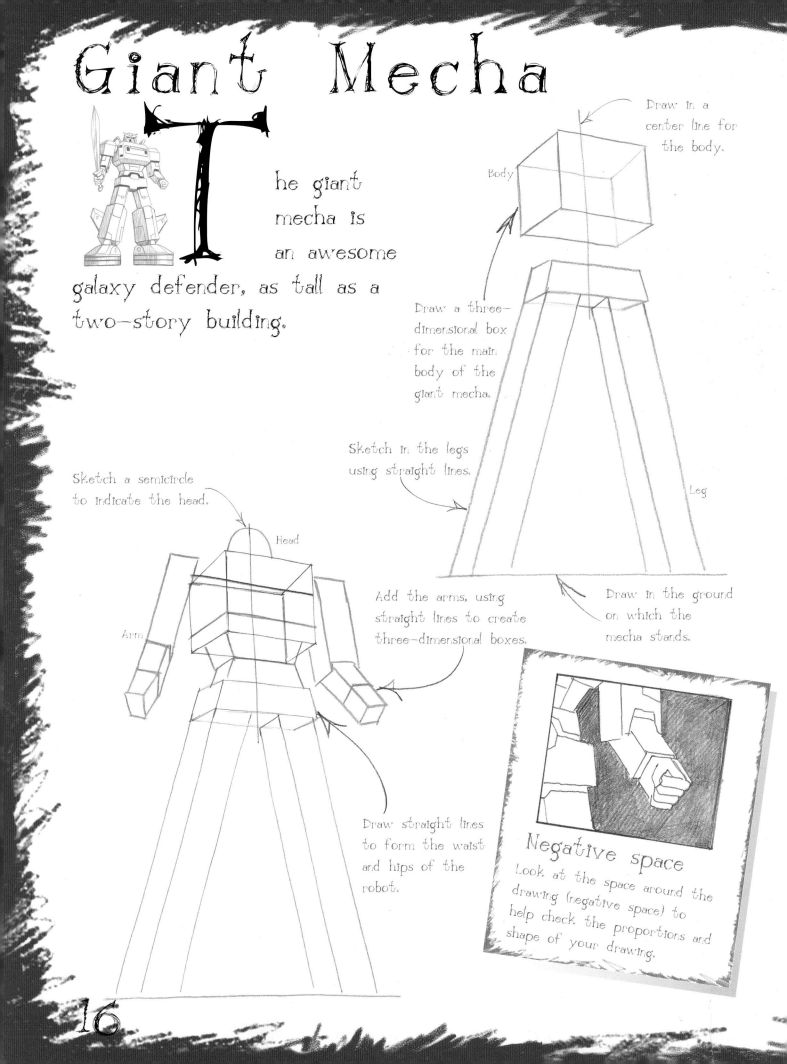

The giant mecha is an awesome galaxy defender, as tall as a two-story building.

Draw in a center line for the body.

Body

Draw a three-dimensional box for the main body of the giant mecha.

Sketch in the legs using straight lines.

Leg

Sketch a semicircle to indicate the head.

Head

Arm

Add the arms, using straight lines to create three-dimensional boxes.

Draw in the ground on which the mecha stands.

Draw straight lines to form the waist and hips of the robot.

Negative space

Look at the space around the drawing (negative space) to help check the proportions and shape of your drawing.

Sketch in the sword.

Sketch the details of the face.

*Remove your construction lines once you are sure you have finished with them.

Add straight lines to the tops of the arms to form the shoulders.

Using your construction lines as a guide, draw in the hands of the mecha.

Finish the detail of the head.

Shade in one side of the sword.

Draw two large rectangles for the base of the feet. Then add the ankle joints and main areas of the leg.

Add the detail to the mecha. Straight lines on its surface show how it is made mechanically.

Decide on where the light is coming from, then shade the areas where it would not reach.

17

Flying Mecha

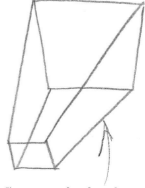

The flying mecha is an aerial combat craft. Its wings and rocket boosters allow it to travel at great speeds and fight any airborne danger.

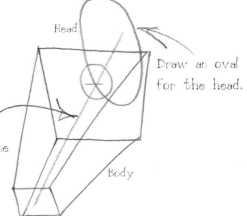

Begin the flying mecha by drawing a simple box in perspective.

Head

Draw an oval for the head.

Draw a center line through the perspective box.

Body

Sketch in straight lines for the shape of the arms.

Add construction lines for the hands.

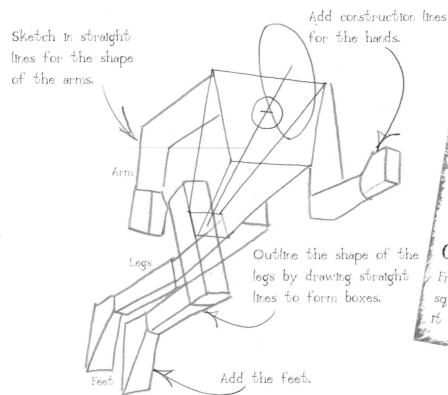

Arm

Legs

Feet

Outline the shape of the legs by drawing straight lines to form boxes.

Add the feet.

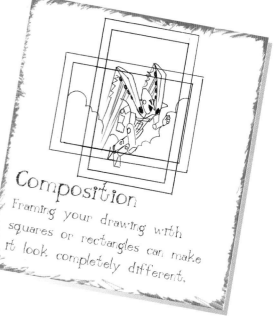

Composition
Framing your drawing with squares or rectangles can make it look completely different.

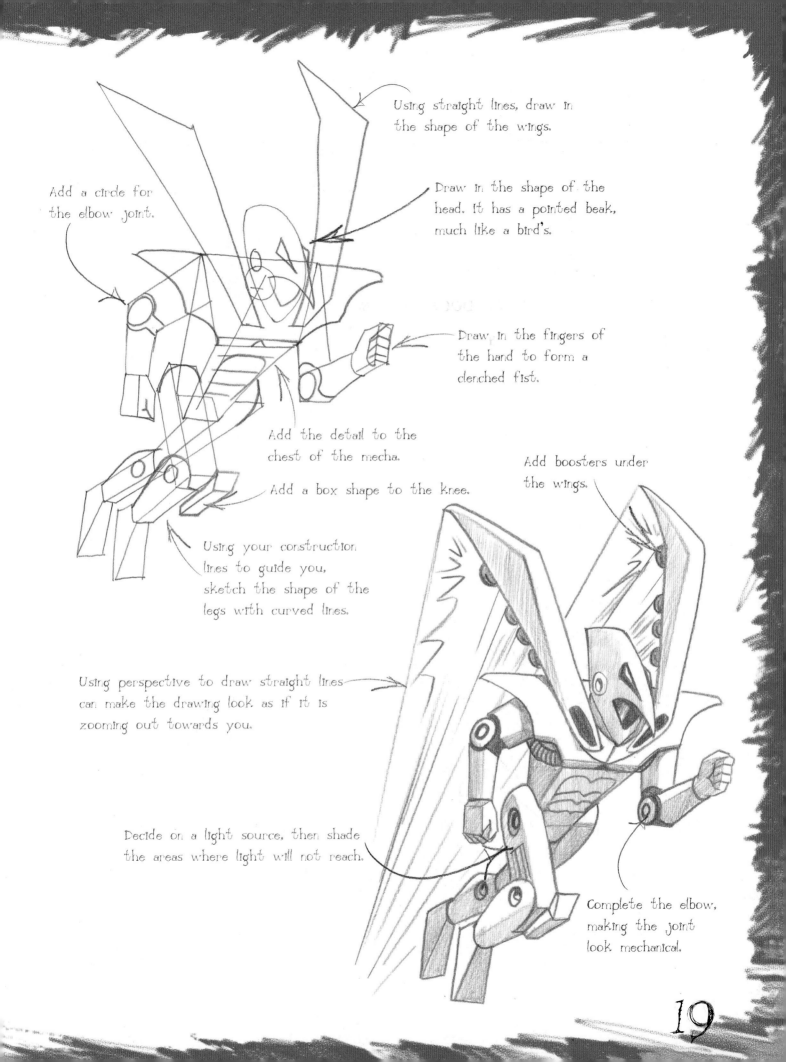

Using straight lines, draw in the shape of the wings.

Draw in the shape of the head. It has a pointed beak, much like a bird's.

Add a circle for the elbow joint.

Draw in the fingers of the hand to form a clenched fist.

Add the detail to the chest of the mecha.

Add boosters under the wings.

Add a box shape to the knee.

Using your construction lines to guide you, sketch the shape of the legs with curved lines.

Using perspective to draw straight lines can make the drawing look as if it is zooming out towards you.

Decide on a light source, then shade the areas where light will not reach.

Complete the elbow, making the joint look mechanical.

19

Explorer Robot

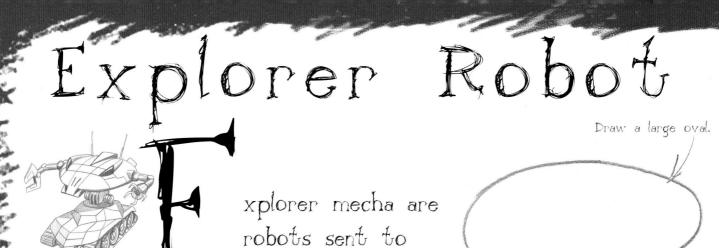

Draw a large oval.

Explorer mecha are robots sent to dangerous worlds all over the galaxy. This one has heavy tank tracks for any type of ground and tools for taking samples from the surface.

Draw a simple perspective box for the base of the exploration robot.

Perspective box

Draw two curved lines going diagonally across the large oval.

The joint between the top of the mecha and the bottom is made up of curved and straight lines.

Draw a line about halfway up the box. Then draw diagonal lines to the top and bottom of the perspective box to form the front end of the explorer mecha.

Draw an oval on the top of the box. Add curved lines from its edges up to a smaller oval.

Add ovals for the wheels, drawing a smaller curved line inside them to make them look three-dimensional.

Track

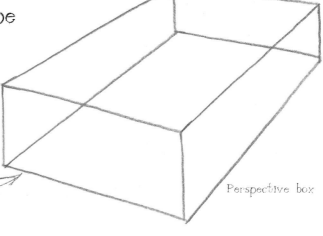

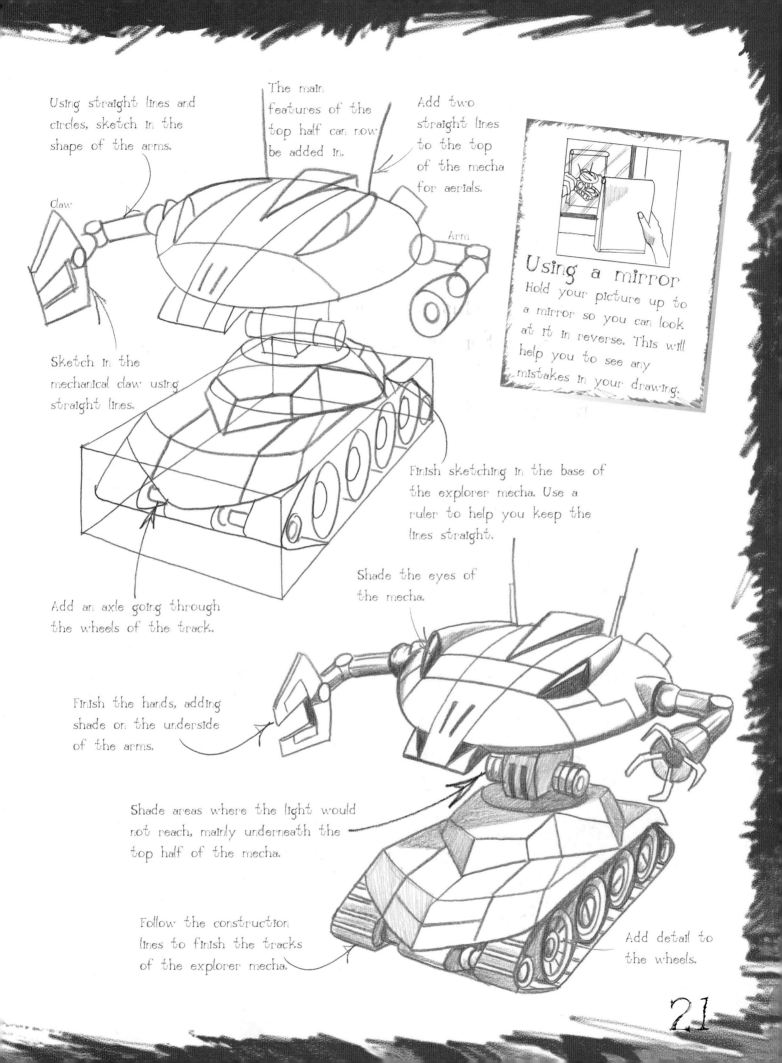

Using straight lines and circles, sketch in the shape of the arms.

Claw

The main features of the top half can now be added in.

Add two straight lines to the top of the mecha for aerials.

Arm

Using a mirror
Hold your picture up to a mirror so you can look at it in reverse. This will help you to see any mistakes in your drawing.

Sketch in the mechanical claw using straight lines.

Finish sketching in the base of the explorer mecha. Use a ruler to help you keep the lines straight.

Add an axle going through the wheels of the track.

Shade the eyes of the mecha.

Finish the hands, adding shade on the underside of the arms.

Shade areas where the light would not reach, mainly underneath the top half of the mecha.

Follow the construction lines to finish the tracks of the explorer mecha.

Add detail to the wheels.

21

Combat Mecha

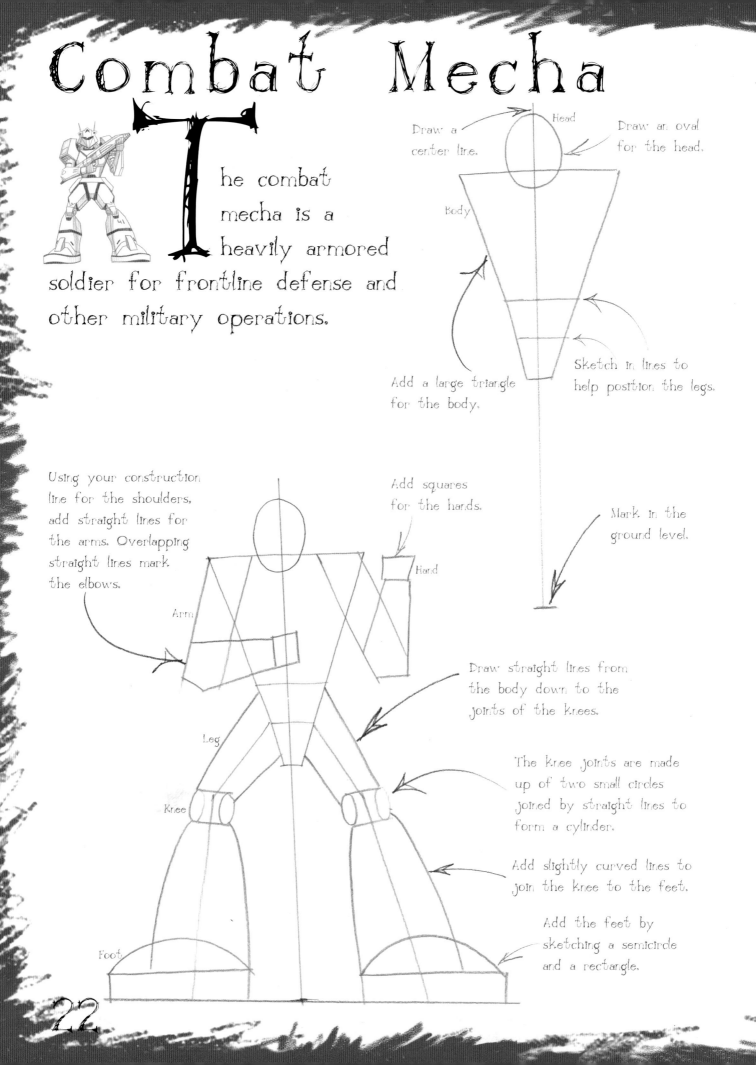

T he combat mecha is a heavily armored soldier for frontline defense and other military operations.

Draw a center line.

Head

Draw an oval for the head.

Body

Add a large triangle for the body.

Sketch in lines to help position the legs.

Using your construction line for the shoulders, add straight lines for the arms. Overlapping straight lines mark the elbows.

Add squares for the hands.

Hand

Mark in the ground level.

Arm

Draw straight lines from the body down to the joints of the knees.

Leg

The knee joints are made up of two small circles joined by straight lines to form a cylinder.

Knee

Add slightly curved lines to join the knee to the feet.

Add the feet by sketching a semicircle and a rectangle.

Foot

22

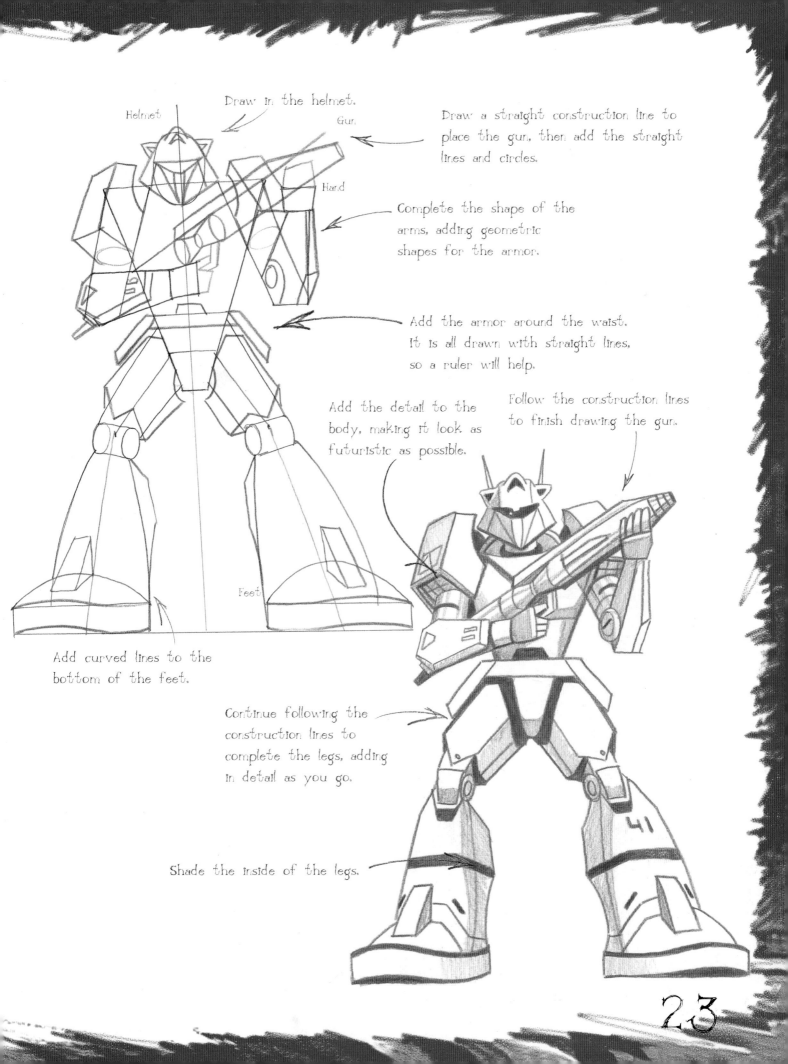

Helmet

Draw in the helmet.

Gun

Draw a straight construction line to place the gun, then add the straight lines and circles.

Hand

Complete the shape of the arms, adding geometric shapes for the armor.

Add the armor around the waist. It is all drawn with straight lines, so a ruler will help.

Add the detail to the body, making it look as futuristic as possible.

Follow the construction lines to finish drawing the gun.

Feet

Add curved lines to the bottom of the feet.

Continue following the construction lines to complete the legs, adding in detail as you go.

Shade the inside of the legs.

23

Human Mecha

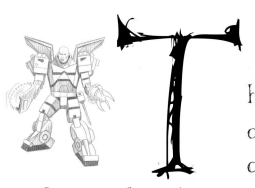

This is a combination of a human and a mecha. It was created with a saw for one hand and a giant claw for the other.

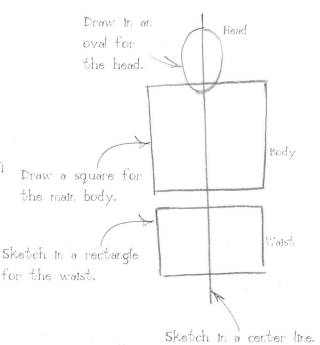

Draw in an oval for the head.

Head

Draw a square for the main body.

Body

Sketch in a rectangle for the waist.

Waist

Sketch in a center line.

Add squares for the shoulders. Connect more rectangles to them for the arms.

Sketch lines for the position of the eyes, nose, and mouth.

Shoulder

Sketch an oval to create a construction line for the claw

Add a large oval for the saw.

Saw

Arm

Draw in the legs using four simple box shapes.

Leg

Foot

The feet are semicircular in construction, so sketch them with curved and straight lines.

Construction lines
Sketching in construction lines helps you create and keep the shape of your drawing. Once the drawing is finished, remove any that are left.

Add wings on the back of the mecha.

Sketch in the detail of the main body. Use straight lines to create a chest and stomach.

Using the construction lines to help, start drawing the mechanical claw.

Add the joint of the leg.

Complete the detail of the face.

Add details to the feet using circles and squares.

Add more detail to the arms to make them look more mechanical.

Add the jagged edge of the saw.

Use the construction lines as a guide to complete the legs.

Finish the claw.

Shade areas where the light will not reach to give the drawing a three-dimensional effect.

Land Walker

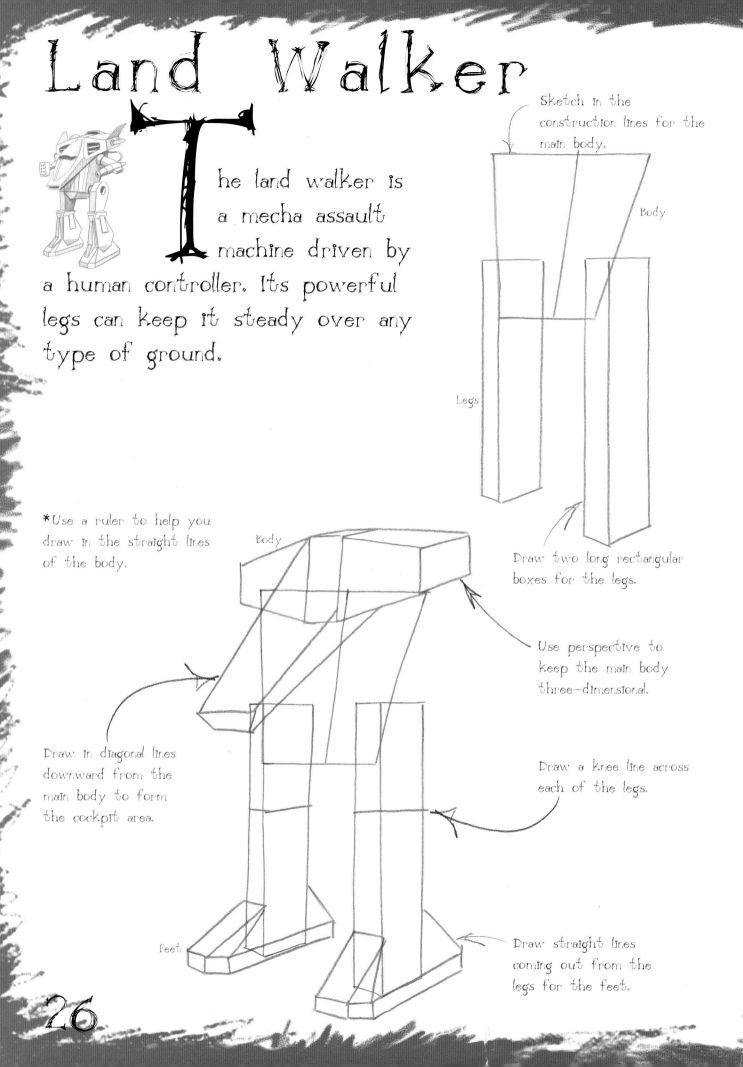

The land walker is a mecha assault machine driven by a human controller. Its powerful legs can keep it steady over any type of ground.

Sketch in the construction lines for the main body.

Body

Legs

Draw two long rectangular boxes for the legs.

Use perspective to keep the main body three-dimensional.

*Use a ruler to help you draw in the straight lines of the body.

Body

Draw in diagonal lines downward from the main body to form the cockpit area.

Draw a knee line across each of the legs.

Draw straight lines coming out from the legs for the feet.

Feet

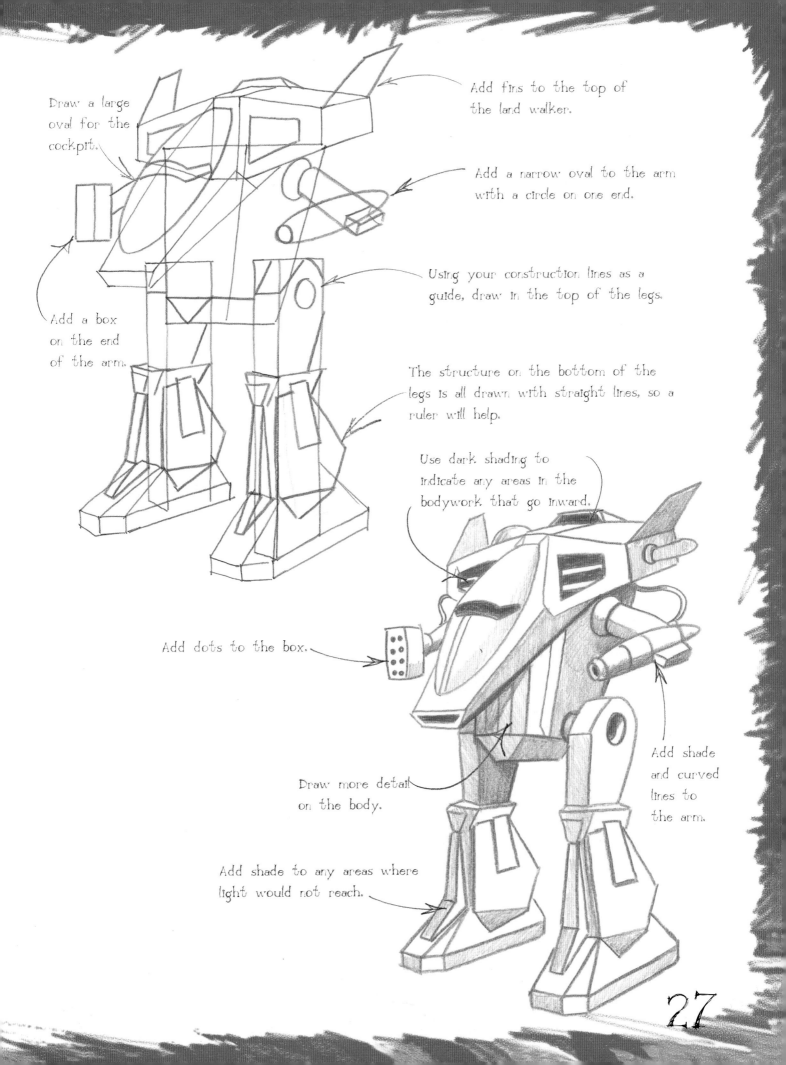

Draw a large oval for the cockpit.

Add fins to the top of the land walker.

Add a narrow oval to the arm with a circle on one end.

Add a box on the end of the arm.

Using your construction lines as a guide, draw in the top of the legs.

The structure on the bottom of the legs is all drawn with straight lines, so a ruler will help.

Use dark shading to indicate any areas in the bodywork that go inward.

Add dots to the box.

Draw more detail on the body.

Add shade and curved lines to the arm.

Add shade to any areas where light would not reach.

27

Mutant Mecha

T he mutant mecha is a giant mechanical monster created by crossing an insect with a robot.

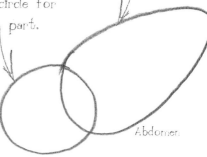

Draw a long egg shape for the rear abdomen.

Sketch a circle for the middle part.

Abdomen

Draw an oval for the head.

Head

Sketch a small circle for the neck.

Chest

Add another circle for the chest.

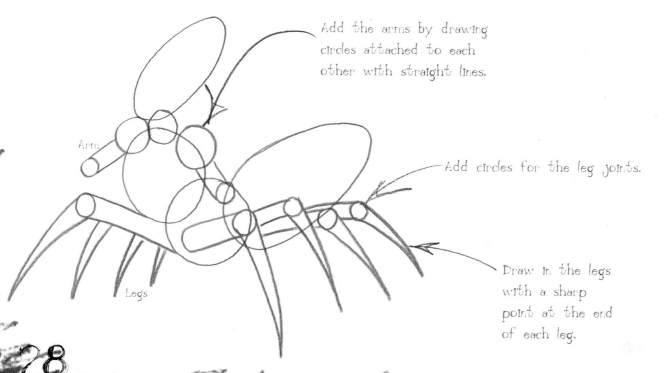

Add the arms by drawing circles attached to each other with straight lines.

Arm

Add circles for the leg joints.

Legs

Draw in the legs with a sharp point at the end of each leg.

Add the eyes.

Draw the shape of the head using curved lines.

Draw in a claw using curved lines.

Add a sharp claw to the rear of the abdomen.

Draw a curved line down from the neck to the body. Use this to help you draw in the chest.

Add the feet.

Add detail to the head.

Draw curved lines on the abdomen to make it look three-dimensional.

Add more detail to the face, shading the eyes.

Shade in the areas where light would not reach.

Finish the detail on the main body.

Add a shaded line to each leg to give them a shiny, metallic look.

29

Fantasy Mecha

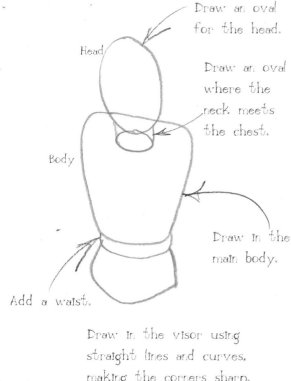

The medieval style of the fantasy mecha takes a knight from the past and mixes it with a robot from the future!

Draw an oval for the head.

Draw an oval where the neck meets the chest.

Head

Body

Draw in the main body.

Add a waist.

Draw in the arms, using circles for the joints and hands.

Draw a straight line for the sword.

Draw in the visor using straight lines and curves, making the corners sharp.

Sketch in curves for the shoulder armor.

Arm

Sword

Hand

Sketch in the legs with straight lines.

Add circles for the knees.

Add circles to the front and side of the knees.

Draw in the lower body armor using curved lines.

Leg

Foot

Draw a simple shape for the feet.

Complete the sword with straight lines for the blade and curves for the handle.

Add the eye slit to the visor.

Add a spike coming from the elbow.

Draw in the armor cuffs with straight lines and curves to make a cone shape.

Sketch in the cape using long, curved lines.

Cape

Draw in the hands using the circular construction lines as guides.

Shade areas of the helmet and visor, to give them a metallic look.

Ankle

Add detail to the ankle areas.

Finish the laser sword.

Finish any detail on the armor and remove any unwanted construction lines.

Add detail to the surface of the armor. Small circles can look like bolts that are holding the armor together.

Shade where light will not reach.

Glossary

chiaroscuro (kee-AHR-uh-skyur-oh) The use of light and dark in a drawing.

composition (kom-puh-ZIH-shun) The positioning of a picture on the drawing paper.

construction lines (kun-STRUK-shun LYNZ) Structural lines used in the early stages of a drawing, and usually erased later.

cross-hatching (KROS-hach-ing) A series of criss-crossing lines used to add shade to a drawing.

fixative (FIK-suh-tiv) A type of resin used to spray over a finished drawing to prevent smudging. It should only be used by an adult.

hatching (HACH-ing) A series of parallel lines used to add shade to a drawing.

light source (LYT SORS) The direction from which the light seems to come in a drawing.

mecha (MEH-ka) Walking robots controlled by a pilot, often appearing in science fiction.

proportion (pruh-POR-shun) The correct relationship of scale between parts of a drawing.

three-dimensional (three-deh-MENCH-nul) Having an effect of depth, so as to look lifelike or real.

Index

Web Sites

Due to the changing nature of Internet links, PowerKids Press has developed an online list of Web sites related to the subject of this book. This site is updated regularly. Please use this link to access the list:

www.powerkidslinks.com/htd/robots/